I Must

Don G. Cyphers
with
W. Bradley Wright

I MUST

Copyright © 2016 by Don G. Cyphers
Published by Stellar Communications Houston

All Rights Reserved. No part of this book may be used or reproduced in any form or by any means, electronic or mechanical, including photocopying, recording, or by any information storage and retrieval systems, without written permission of the copyright owner. For information, contact Stellar Communications Houston.

All Biblical quotes reference the King James Version of the Bible.

First Edition: May 2016
Printed in the United States of America.

I Must

ISBN-10: 1-944952-06-3
ISBN-13: 978-1-944952-06-8

Stellar Communications Houston
www.stellarwriter.com
281.804.7089

Written with W. Bradley Wright
Preparation for publication by Ella Hearrean Ritchie
Cover art by Robert R. Jones
Interior formatting by Elena Reznikova

Introduction

I Must

In every Christian's Walk, there comes a time when the Father summons his children back to the flock. It is a very specific call that ripples through the universe and ignites our souls when we are directed to follow Jesus.

As we prepare for our wonderful journey together, it is important to be mindful of the blessings in our lives, but even more so, the lessons we have learned from loss. It is in the darkest depths of our pain that God begins our transformation.

I know because I have been there, caught in a vortex of paralyzing fear while faced with the whole of my inner demons. I was bloodied and bruised in the fight for my life, but the Spirit kept me unbowed. He met me in the pitch black and revealed how vital His light truly is, was, and always will be. Grace is the only reason I was able to emerge from the rubble and tell the tale.

In my refinement, He revealed an encrypted truth in **I Kings 13** *that has been overlooked, and I feel called to share with you and the rest of the world: use the story of Jeroboam and the nameless prophet to sharpen students' pastoral strengths by drawing from their lessons learned in catastrophe. By tapping into this Spiritual source, it will equip our future church leaders with the ability to deliver the Word with a never-before-seen potency.*

The following pages are an expression of the power behind **I Kings 13** *coupled with places in my life where God protected and directed my arrival into His glory. I feel that the Word and my story will help Him carve a place in others' hearts to kindle the same sense of urgency that was stamped into mine, and it can only be summed up in the two words:* **I Must**.

This book is dedicated to my lovely wife of many years, Debra Y. Cyphers; my mother, Lillian "Baby Ree" McCullough; the sweet members of the Strait Gate Fellowship Baptist Church of Elgin, Texas (Wild Cat Country); and my family and friends who supported and encouraged me over the years.

I Must

Don G. Cyphers
with
W. Bradley Wright

INTRODUCTION	3
CHAPTER ONE: **The Call**	7
CHAPTER TWO: **It's All in the Preparation, Prayer, and the Power**	15
CHAPTER THREE: **The Challenge**	25
CHAPTER FOUR: **Seems Like Confidence**	29
CHAPTER FIVE: **Decisions, Decisions, Decisions...**	33
CHAPTER SIX: **Listen and Obey**	37
CHAPTER SEVEN: **Trick or Truth**	41
CHAPTER EIGHT: **The Way It's Played**	45
CHAPTER NINE: **Lies, Lies, Lies**	53
CHAPTER TEN: **What If?**	57
CHAPTER ELEVEN: **Playing the Fool**	61
CHAPTER TWELVE: **Where is the Finish Line?**	65

I Must

I Kings 13:1-7

1 And, behold, there came a man of God out of Judah by the word of the Lord unto Bethel: and Jeroboam stood by the altar to burn incense.

2 And he cried against the altar in the word of the Lord, and said, O altar, altar, thus saith the Lord; Behold, a child shall be born unto the house of David, Josiah by name; and upon thee shall he offer the priests of the high places that burn incense upon thee, and men's bones shall be burnt upon thee.

3 And he gave a sign the same day, saying, This is the sign which the Lord hath spoken; Behold, the altar shall be rent, and the ashes that are upon it shall be poured out.

4 And it came to pass, when king Jeroboam heard the saying of the man of God, which had cried against the altar in Bethel, that he put forth his hand from the altar, saying, Lay hold on him. And his hand, which he put forth against him, dried up, so that he could not pull it in again to him.

5 The altar also was rent, and the ashes poured out from the altar, according to the sign which the man of God had given by the word of the Lord.

6 And the king answered and said unto the man of God, Intreat now the face of the Lord thy God, and pray for me, that my hand may be restored me again. And the man of God besought the Lord, and the king's hand was restored him again, and became as it was before.

7 And the king said unto the man of God, Come home with me, and refresh thyself, and I will give thee a reward.

CHAPTER ONE

The Call

I Kings 13:1-7

We begin with a breakdown of the Scripture that will be guiding our way. We will work to understand some of its basic ideas and couple them with lessons I have learned along the way to provide a clear vision of what it looks like to accept the Call.

While Jeroboam was preparing for a sacrifice, a prophet from Judah appeared in the city of Bethel, which translates to: "The house of God." At the time, Bethel was a far cry from its name and was in desperate need of healing. That healing process began when a nameless prophet stopped King Jeroboam from desecrating the Lord's altar by proclaiming the Word of the Lord. Jeroboam was enraged at the sound of an alien commanding him to stop his ritual. He furiously commanded his men to seize the prophet by pointing at the Lord's servant. With his arm fully extended and trembling with anger, it suddenly began to go limp. Quickly, the limp appendage began to decay until it was completely withered and dead.

The king was horrified. His arm was dead, and worse, his power was dying with it. Jeroboam then desperately commanded the prophet to prove his holy communion with God by performing the miracle that would bring the king's arm back to life. The prophet humbly obliged, and the king's arm returned to its former state. Jeroboam was elated with the return of his arm and his power. The king then made every attempt to shower the prophet with gifts. The prophet was offered every possible luxury, but the prophet refused. He had been given orders from God to simply pass through Bethel, deliver the Word, and reject all forms of hospitality. He held firm to his orders and made it through the first challenge by standing firm in the Lord. It was not to be his last, however.

In order for the prophet to perform such works, he had to be given a Call. To be Called is to be uprooted from day-to-day life and placed on a path specifically paved to carry out the will of the Lord.

I Must

Hearing the Call carries a tremendous amount of power and must be feared because it is God's activation of the Spirit in us to do His will. As such, the Lord of Hosts gave the prophet his Call to deliver a convicting word for Jeroboam. As the king's arm began to die in defiance of the Word, it personified the mortality we all face when walking in disobedience. The incapacitating terror he felt was the result of his singed spirit reacting to the Word's burning principle lit by the fire of Jehovah. Jeroboam's tune quickly flipped from rage to grace after he was healed and said, "Entreat now the face of the Lord thy God." This was a man, a king who had gone his own way in outright defiance of the Law. He was consumed with power, and even if only for a moment, we see him bent before the Throne.

When navigating through hard circumstances, it brings to mind the passage of **Isaiah 46:10** that tells us "(God) sees the end from the beginning." That means that every action God sets in motion is done with a specific destination in mind. We see this in the prophet when the king advanced on him and offered forbidden rewards. To even be in that situation, he had to journey all the way from Judah to Bethel in order to proclaim the Word. That tells me the Lord was with the prophet, and the prophet had clearly been a recipient of the Lord's abounding love that continually provides for those who work His ministry. In the case of the prophet, his ministry was following his Call. Just as it carried him to the moment for which he was Called, he had to remain committed to his Call in order to complete his mission. In other words, he had to continue to obey.

It was through that obedience that the Lord spoke through the prophet with a resounding No! That was the first step he needed to complete in order to fulfill his Call. All Calls are moved closer to being fulfilled when we hear His voice flow out of our mouths. We must remain obedient throughout our Call's pursuit because it is the means to His ends, and not ours.

Let's take a look at the nameless prophet. I believe that the prophet remained nameless because he represents us. He is any person willing to submit his or her life to expanding the Kingdom. Anyone with that kind of heart has the ability to receive the Call. His obedience and effective execution of the Lord's will was more than an order fulfilled; it was a life-giving boost, and it is our example. His mission could just as easily have been given to anyone else who chose the path of righteousness, but it was given to him just as ours is given to us. The prophet filled his lungs with the precious breath

Chapter One: The Call

of life by wholly living in obedience. He experienced the profound, ornate beauty of the Spirit by simply obeying. Our walk and our obedience put us under the Lord's provision and protection where, under His wing, He places us on His time.

When gifted with that celestial pocket watch, we must not sit and wait. If we do, it can cause us to fall into a slumber that invites the wicked snares of our own brokenness in the way Bethel did to so many others who were walking in disobedience. Those snares will keep us on the wrong time, with the wrong provisions, amongst the wrong people, and dying the wrong way at the hands of horrible consequence. Our Call is to go to and through the places we are to heal, and we are to execute according to His time and provision. The fruit of our execution yields as we deliver the will of the Lord through the invigorated obedience of **I Must** that gives us our drive and, more importantly, our name in Him.

I believe in my heart that the true Call from God ignites an eternal flame that burns brighter and brighter with every achievement. One of the most important elements often forgotten in our church leaders today is that we forget what gave us our initial fire—that visceral drive to pursue the Great Commission. He shows us the way and equips us with what we need, and the beauty of it is that all of it is channeled through our free will. That means that the only force that can ignite or extinguish the blaze in our hearts boils down to the choice between His will or ours.

I Kings 13 shows us that as we grow closer to God, He gives us a vision and plants a passion in our hearts to pursue His ends. No matter the size of the task, following His Call enters us into perfect relationship with the Father. He prunes the young believer with every step taken by His side. Over time, more and more spiritual fruit will be gained, and with each growing bounty, the yield begins to develop an essential level of confidence and faith that cuts the cornerstone of obedience. Each time we surmount adversity and taste the faintest hint of victory, our faith and confidence fuse into a bigger and brighter force that explodes into an assortment of vibrant self-efficacy. It is something so brilliant that the undeniable force inspires men and women from all walks of life to drop everything and join the Mission. **I Kings 13** establishes this in a unique light, and we will discover the first step in **I Must** begins with the Call.

This Call—how wonderful and universal, and if achieved, how triumphant in the life of the servant.

I Must

When God Calls us, He is very clear when He says that he will directly speak with words, visions, and/or dreams. The root of God's desire to reach out to his children began in **Numbers 12:4-8** when He came to Moses, Miriam, and Aaron:

> **4** *And the Lord spake suddenly unto Moses, and unto Aaron, and unto Miriam, Come out ye three unto the tabernacle of the congregation. And they three came out.* **5** *And the Lord came down in the pillar of the cloud, and stood in the door of the tabernacle, and called Aaron and Miriam: and they both came forth.* **6** *And he said, Hear now my words: If there be a prophet among you, I the Lord will make myself known unto him in a vision, and will speak unto him in a dream.* **7** *My servant Moses is not so, who is faithful in all mine house.* **8** *With him will I speak mouth to mouth, even apparently, and not in dark speeches; and the similitude of the Lord shall he behold: wherefore then were ye not afraid to speak against my servant Moses?*

I can plainly recall the dream when the Lord visited me. It was so beautiful and so clear. He shook me awake and opened my eyes to a light so powerful and so bright that it outshone the noonday sun. It was there He told me to go and preach the Word. He said it three times. I'll never forget it. Straight out of **Matthew 11:29** and plain as day, "Learn of me and go and tell all the world."

I'll be honest, there are some days when I just don't want to preach, I don't want to teach, and I don't want to lead. Yet every time I fall to the enemy, the *I Must* within me violently stirs and forces me to follow my instructions in a way that rings of Paul's summons on the Damascus road.

Similarly, when we met the nameless prophet, he was following the fire of the Call to go to Bethel. The commission he followed is the same that has been charged to us: to pursue the world with all of our hearts. Our time here is very short and the door is closing fast. There has to be a sense of urgency as we seek to fulfill our mission in the same way Paul's relentless drive was awakened after experiencing his Call on the road to Damascus. There was absolutely no hesitation when he recognized that it was God in his supplication: "And he trembling and astonished said, Lord, what wilt thou have me to do? And the Lord said unto him, Arise, and go into the city, and it shall be told thee what thou must do (**Acts 9:6**)."

CHAPTER ONE: **The Call**

Then in **Acts 9:9-14**, we see where Paul's scales were removed from his eyes and the *I Must* enlightened his soul:

> **9** *And he was three days without sight, and neither did eat nor drink.* **10** *And there was a certain disciple at Damascus, named Ananias; and to him said the Lord in a vision, Ananias. And he said, Behold, I am here, Lord.* **11** *And the Lord said unto him, Arise, and go into the street which is called Straight, and enquire in the house of Judas for one called Saul, of Tarsus: for, behold, he prayeth,* **12** *And hath seen in a vision a man named Ananias coming in, and putting his hand on him, that he might receive his sight.* **13** *Then Ananias answered, Lord, I have heard by many of this man, how much evil he hath done to thy saints at Jerusalem:* **14** *And here he hath authority from the chief priests to bind all that call on thy name.*

He had no way to deny the conviction that he must go and achieve the goals of the Lord. In the exact same way, we will have to recognize the beginnings of *I Must* in our Call.

As we continue through **I Kings 13**, we learn where the man of God was sent from and where he was headed: from Judah to Bethel. Throughout the Pentateuch and the book of Samuel, Bethel is described as a very prominent and influential community filled with pomp and excess—dangerous vices for weakened flesh. As those vices were then, so are they today, and every single one of us has a Bethel to heal.

Scripture takes us to where Jeroboam is working around the altar—a place where he had absolutely no business being. He was a corrupted king, not an anointed priest; altars are holy places where God proves his Word. Jeroboam was told that the altar was already desecrated due to the fact that he allowed dead men's bones to be sacrificed instead of the flesh of animals that God had commanded. Because of that desecration, the priests' inactions, and the old priests' willful defiance, we find the whole city collectively desecrated. The unsanitary effects of sacrificing human remains had spread all over the city; this is the reason why the man of God was not allowed to eat or accept any form of hospitality. Every resource was contaminated.

In order to set Bethel's restoration in motion, the prophet had to go to the source—the altar and the king. When God spoke through

I Must

the prophet, Jeroboam's infected hubris rejected the word of the Lord and the man who shared it, and his consequence was a taste of death. In showing this flash of death, Scripture is using another way to tell us that disobedience, ignorant of repentance, is the source of our sin and failures that kill us until we learn to listen.

I remember after my Call, one of the dreams that truly anointed my power, the inner power of my deepest strengths, was about a loaf of bread. No kidding. I was told in my dream that I would receive the loaf of bread for the feeding of the people with the bread of life. I remember when I woke up, I looked over at my wife, and she was the first to hear my announcement. I sat and thought, and with each passing second I felt a power that I had never felt begin to swell and spring from within. I stepped outside to my driveway to get some fresh air, and I saw my uncle walking up. I could tell that he was carrying something but couldn't make out what it was. But the closer he got, the more I just smiled as it became clearer that a loaf of bread was swaying in the morning sun. He came up to me and handed over the bread saying, "I don't know why I am doing this, but I was told in my spirit to bring you a loaf of bread."

I told my uncle, Andrew was his name, that God called me to preach with a loaf of bread. We just looked at one another for a brief moment and then burst out and rejoiced. I called my pastor and told him that one loaf of bread gave me the sign to go out and share the Word. Experiences like this one show us that signs follow the true Call. These signs are given to insert spiritual power over the individual. No sign? No Call. Signs are not to be boasted upon, but they do become testimonies, which are the fiery moments and truths from individuals' stories that provide sound evidence of changes in their lives.

Those moments are small glimpses of what it is to experience the full view of Jesus and His Transfiguration mentioned in **Matthew 17:1–9**, **Mark 9:2-8**, and **Luke 9:28–36**. Remember, testimonies are truths, not lies. If it is not a sign, it will die. They are also not for bragging about, but they are designed to propel individuals in their respective walks.

One of the first examples of God showing up in this way is found in **Exodus 3:1-10**, when Moses was given his orders to confront Pharaoh through the sign of the burning bush. I cannot stress enough that signs are paramount for the Call. If the sign has providential evidence, one might see something similar to Jeroboam's

CHAPTER ONE: **The Call**

hand dying in disobedience, or a burning bush speaking Truth to confront a horrible ruler. So when it comes down to it, folks will ask what my evidence was. The bread I received was very real, and it came straight from the voice of God. In order to discern our gifts, we must have signs and evidence. Just as the scales on Paul's eyes in **Acts 9** were his evidence, Joshua's final sign was given by a man waving a sword on the road to Jericho in **Joshua 5:13-15**.

The Call is the most important event in our development as believers because it builds our purpose in Him. **I Kings 13** shows how the prophet followed his Call to save a people and to correct a king, and it was just as vital an expression of God's grace then as it is now. By submitting to the Word, delivering a sign, and refusing hospitality, we see God moving through the nameless prophet's obedience. As such, before we can be equipped to perform a similar task, we, too, must feel the flame of the Call, discern its origins, and prepare to perform the task—that's where the real work begins.

Chapter Two

It's All in the Preparation, Prayer, and the Power

Matthew 28:19-20

19 *Go ye therefore, and teach all nations, baptizing them in the name of the Father, and of the Son, and of the Holy Ghost:*

20 *Teaching them to observe all things whatsoever I have commanded you: and, lo, I am with you always, even unto the end of the world. Amen.*

Upon accepting the Call, we must be prepared to answer it. That answer comes through prayer, where we open ourselves to hear the promise that God has placed upon our hearts. We will be exploring a variety of biblical and personal examples to further clarify what that means in *I Must*.

Before any spiritual event can be carried out by a soldier of the Kingdom, there must be a pure conference with God in the holy communion of prayer. Through that precious connection, God gives us our orders. This connection is the source for everything that is designed for our lives. Sincere prayer is the way of life. In walking with *I Must*, *I Must* pray always—it is an absolute must because prayer is about fellowshipping with Him. More specifically, it is the truest expression of fellowship with God. Communing in fervent prayer emboldens our purpose and strengthens our walk with Him.

I Kings describes Jeroboam standing next to an altar preparing for sacrifice when his ritual is interrupted by the approaching man of God. The timing was such that both men were at the altar. One was righteous and the other was not. What is so beautiful is that God knew both men's hearts. Before anything could happen, the prophet had to bow before the private altar of his heart before carrying out the Lord's orders to confront Jeroboam.

When we engage with the Lord in preparatory prayer, He releases the strength and courage necessary to confront any and all challenges. One wonders how frightened the prophet must have been to even approach the king. In order to be that spiritually armored, he had no other way of executing his mission other than to be prayerfully prepared. The fears that must have raced through his mind: Was his language in order? His diction? The protocols? His ethics? There are an infinite number of mental hang-ups and doubts that drive individuals insane before executing a vision. Through obedience, the prophet exemplified the fact that God will never allow any of His called to stand to be unprepared before any trial. It's the same way Moses was prepared to stand before Pharaoh. He was conditioned and primed for his heroic feat from infancy. Every day was a step and a lesson. Every moment, every breath, every pain, and every triumph groomed him for the moment when he turned to the man who had given him everything and defiantly demanded the liberation of God's chosen. There will come a time of need, a need for Moses-like strength. The source for fulfilling that need is the Holy Spirit through prayer. Jesus's strength in the wilderness personifies this in **Luke 4:1-2**: "And Jesus being full of the Holy Ghost returned from Jordan, and was led by the Spirit into the wilderness, **2** Being forty days tempted of the devil. And in those days he did eat nothing: and when they were ended, he afterward hungered."

It is abundantly clear Jesus was in the midst of prayer. He had to have been to triumph over Satan in the fiercest challenge that anyone could ever imagine. The Prince of Hell was upon God's son. Just think about that for a second. Satan, bent on destroying every blessed thing on the planet, has the opportunity to attack God's only Son, and fails! Jesus's war within cannot even be fathomed, but Scripture shows us that His strength came directly from the Lord on the wings of an angel in **Matthew 4:11**: "Then the devil leaveth him, and, behold, angels came and ministered unto him." In order to receive that kind of strength in that exact moment, prayer is the only way. Just as it was for Jesus and His preceding prophets, including the nameless prophet from **I Kings**, prayer is vital.

Prayer is a mighty method that works in powerful ways, and there must be three things: there must be a purpose, there must be embrace, and there must be praise.

When building upon the Call, one must pray about the purpose. Then one must embrace the purpose. Finally, one must give praise to God for the purpose. These three elements have to be set in order

Chapter Two: It's All in the Preparation, Prayer, and the Power

to fully initiate the *"I Must."*

The purpose is the mandate that God has laid upon us. All of us have one. How we choose to approach achieving that purpose is what makes or breaks us in our respective walks with the Lord. ***I Must*** fulfills that purpose. To achieve the pure purpose of God, we have to allow ourselves to be instruments and messengers of His plan. As we do that, we must communicate with Him in prayer where He opens up our eyes, ears, and mouth. He quickens our spirit to achieve His purpose. In the middle of this, to don His encouragement, we must embrace our purpose. We must have a passion for the purpose that rages with love, sincerity, obligation, and they must be full in our hearts before bending our knee to the Throne. If we do not, failure is the only viable outcome as God will not tolerate lukewarm effort. If one is to embark on this incredible adventure, it's all or nothing.

Embrace is expressed in a number of ways throughout our day-to-day lives. For example, it is expressed when a man truly embraces the woman he loves, or in a handshake between friends where a simple touch can enliven the whole body. When we truly embrace His purpose, it energizes us knowing that we are unapologetically accomplishing God's plan for our lives. As we carry that energy, inevitably, opposing forces will crop up. With the armor of God, we can rest in the knowledge that nothing can defeat us. In that war, when we can feel our fight driving us to victory, there must be a prayerful praise by simply thanking Him. **Ephesians 6:10-19** shows us what that armor looks like:

> **10** *Finally, my brethren, be strong in the Lord, and in the power of his might.* **11** *Put on the whole armour of God, that ye may be able to stand against the wiles of the devil.* **12** *For we wrestle not against flesh and blood, but against principalities, against powers, against the rulers of the darkness of this world, against spiritual wickedness in high [places].* **13** *Wherefore take unto you the whole armour of God, that ye may be able to withstand in the evil day, and having done all, to stand.* **14** *Stand therefore, having your loins girt about with truth, and having on the breastplate of righteousness;* **15** *And your feet shod with the preparation of the gospel of peace;* **16** *Above all, taking the shield of faith, wherewith ye shall be able to quench all the fiery darts of the wicked.* **17** *And take the helmet of salvation, and the sword of*

the Spirit, which is the word of God: **18** *Praying always with all prayer and supplication in the Spirit, and watching thereunto with all perseverance and supplication for all saints;* **19** *And for me, that utterance may be given unto me, that I may open my mouth boldly, to make known the mystery of the gospel.*

After prayer, God begins crafting us by showing up in our ministry and in our personal walk. Whenever and wherever He uses us, it engages all of our capabilities. He always meets us where we are and makes the best of what we have. In Exodus, when Moses was shying from his call, he claimed he was slow to speak. God knew his needs and gave him Aaron. Likewise, one of my dear friends has a speech impediment, but when he stands to preach, his voice is clear as day. In these moments, we see God's over-arching theme of mending the broken to change the world.

After showing up in our lives and ministries, God gets to work ensuring we have a clear grasp of the Word. This is evident in **I Kings 13:7**, when the prophet clearly had a firm working knowledge by being able to confront an extremely powerful man with no hesitation. There comes a time that we have to know exactly what we know, and how to deliver it. **II Timothy 2:15** teaches us that we have to rightly divide the meaning of the truth when he says, "Study to shew thyself approved unto God, a workman that needeth not to be ashamed, rightly dividing the word of truth." Before we practice sharing the word, even before a child, we have to dig and research; we have to know what we are saying and that it is totally true. It can't be aimless or off the top of our heads. It must be ensured beyond a shadow of a doubt that the message is thoroughly known because the nations are at stake.

When we are empowered with the knowledge of the Word, we are emboldened to share the Good News. People feed off of the Gospel. People thirst after righteousness when it is prepared in stunning array. When we begin to take in the subtle hints of love in God's call to preparation, it smells sweet, but it must be presented with boldness. At this point in our journey, empty words fall short. There is no longer room for wasted air that promises nothing. The steps must be followed by actions. The emphasis in this portion of Scripture shows us that the prophet's preparation was specifically designed by God. The man showed up in Bethel out of nowhere without advertising his actions; he just did what he was called to do.

CHAPTER TWO: It's All in the Preparation, Prayer, and the Power

It is my firm belief that when people do too much talking, they ruin things. Loose lips sink ships; big thunder, no lightning. So we find this prophet was surely prepared for the work of the Lord.

The prophet's Call was Spirit-led, and it equipped him to answer and fulfill what he was called to do. At the heart of this, listening and following the steps that prepared us to execute the Call remain vital to our approach. God gives to those who are prepared. If we are not prepared, we are a liability. All of us have a purpose or drive behind what we are called to accomplish. That purpose is developed during the equipping stage. Little preparedness, light work. Big preparedness, mighty work. You can preach, and maybe teach to thousands of people, but if you learn to put it to paper, you can reach millions. It's all in the preparation.

One of the greatest teachers in the Bible, the Apostle Paul was prepared to share his work in front of all the world. It didn't matter if he was a beggar or a king. He was prepared and used by God to share the Word all over Asia Minor. Similarly, Moses was prepared in the unique way of sitting at the table of the Pharaoh, receiving the best education available and living in luxury. He spent forty years living it up under the rule of Pharaoh, then forty more years leading sheep. These very different times brought Moses into a deep relationship with the Lord. They prepared him to eloquently translate God's instruction into the Pentateuch. Just as Paul and Moses were developed through a very specific set of circumstances that were tailored to them and their strengths, so are we in today's time.

In my Call, He said, "Learn of me." He didn't just tell me to get going. He said, "Learn of me."

When we take on the responsibility of learning about our God, His Spirit fills us with His knowledge. That prepares us to share it with whomever we come into contact. One of the hardest lessons I learned taught me about preparation. I thought I had prepared myself as thoroughly as possible for an exam. I was walking tall, just resting in how prepared I knew I was. On my way in, I stopped in the doorway to pray. I stood there, in the middle of the doorway, and asked God to give me the required strength to wield my unsurpassed knowledge of the Word. While in prayer, I could feel the presence of another figure approaching me, and much to my surprise it was not Jesus. My moment with God ended abruptly by my professor's subtle voice telling me I was disrupting the class by praying. I apologized and headed to my seat thinking I was in the clear.

I Must

As I took my seat, that figure lingered still, and had the audacity to ask me if I had studied the night before. I beamed with confidence as I replied with all my heart that I had fully prepared for his exam. Then he asked me, "Did you not only study last night, but last week also?" The balloon inside my chest popped. "Did you prepare yourself this week and last week to take this test?" My smile was replaced by sorrow as I faded into my chair. "Let me tell you something," he said. "God helps those who help themselves."

"If you didn't give Him anything to work with, how can He help you?" It made me question whether or not I was as prepared as I thought I was. It makes me wonder, too, was the **I Kings** prophet prepared? The lesson I learned carried over to the Baptist Bible College in Shreveport, Louisiana. I met many great individuals who were in school to learn about the Lord just as I was. Like most, I desperately hoped one day to be able to be used by God. I had no idea it would be on my graduation day. I will never forget it. I was given an opportunity to speak to my graduating class. I had followed a random surge of inspiration and written a sermon a few days before, and, of course, I was asked to speak. It was a message full of faith from **Acts 6:8**.

The Lord was clearly with me the whole way because that message attracted several invitations to preach in churches all over the nation. It clearly had nothing to do with me or my work. It had everything to do with God and the preparation that He bestowed upon me. God came to me in a dream right after my speech and showed me the church for which he wanted me to apply. I followed the instructions. I had some very excellent interviews, but the leaders of that particular church chose another. I felt deep in my spirit that they had chosen the wrong man, and I told them as much. In either case, God later showed up in their business meeting. After several deliberations, it turned out that the man they had chosen over me was stripped of his candidacy. They were left to search on without a secure pastor in their immediate sight. God had other plans. His preparing lessons put me in the best possible place I could be.

None of God's Called will ever enter battle without armor, and, as such, the prophet was guided to stand before the king. He was a man from nowhere, no name, no friends, no anything. We see him stand before one of the most powerful men of that time in humble confidence, which is the only confidence that comes from being personally chosen and equipped by the hand of God. Could he talk or

Chapter Two: It's All in the Preparation, Prayer, and the Power

relate in any way to the king? Could he say something that would catch the king's attention? Could he help the king with his feeble words? No, all he had was the fire of *"I Must."*

God's equipping will give us His desire to set personal goals to His ends. We learn and grow from each successful step we take with Him. In our growth, we begin to recognize a level of competency that is called self-efficacy. That self-efficacy is the swelling power of the One guiding our steps. In this life, we are either moving forward or backward, and forward is our only option. That is why our sensory organs face forward. Our eyes, nose, and mouth are for absorbing what's in front of us while our backside is designed for what needs to be left behind.

When we look at the example of the prophet, we see where he faced his challenge. With his eyes focused on the king, he bravely and humbly delivered the Lord's message (**I Kings 13:1-7**). That triumph is the product of the power of *I Must*.

Philippians 4:13 famously announces, "I can do all things through Christ which strengtheneth me." In *I Must*, we have to recognize our strengths and weaknesses before we accept the role in life we are to play. The Word defines those perimeters, and Its power is very real. While we are praying through our preparation, the Word will come alive in us to drive us through our victories as well as our challenges. As Paul mentions in **I Corinthians**, power is derived directly from our relationship with Jesus Christ and the Word of God, the same source of *I Must*. The **I Kings 13** prophet exemplifies this power by having been in prayer, following through in his preparation, and executing the will of the Lord at the exact moment he was called upon: "And he cried against the altar in the word of the Lord, and said, O altar, altar, thus saith the Lord; Behold, a child shall be born unto the house of David, Josiah by name; and upon thee shall he offer the priests of the high places that burn Incense upon thee, and men's bones shall be burnt upon thee (**I Kings 13:2**)."

Just as prayer is vital to execution, folly is inevitable when we neglect it and the power it brings. My triumphs had nothing to do with physical strength, but rather spiritual strength. If we are right with God first, our bodies will be spiritual conductors through which His power is to flow. When we submit ourselves at the foot of the Throne, it unburdens our spirit. Its power will move through us to heal, embolden, and inspire His strength in us. Some feel that they can "pull themselves up by their own bootstraps," but God is always

I Must

sovereign over the peaks and valleys of our lives. In order to reach those high heights, I believe that, yes, we do make the climb, but without the Lord's anointed power of *I Must*, we will never reach the ultimate glory He has planned for us. In *I Must*, it is the Word that enriches our power. We must be prayerful and prepared to receive it. Upon accepting our power, we must then dive into the Word with full purpose. We must take in the Word so that we have it firmly in our hearts in order to accomplish our personal task.

In 1982, I had the opportunity to cater a frisbee competition at a large park in Austin, Texas. There were masses of people and a sea of advertising representatives with products scattered all about the park. I was blessed with the opportunity to feed them all with barbecue, and I was the only one they called to cook it. I prepared an immense amount of meat. I began by picking up everything I was going to need and laying out my cutlery. From there, I went to town. I remember cooking up two, three, four briskets. I chopped them up really fine and stored them in a big five-gallon pot on the stove.

While I was setting everything up, I was waiting on my wife to bring the food. It was just before we were set to serve when she arrived with everything I needed, or so I thought. As I was unloading the car, my heart rose to my throat—I didn't see any of the pots. I looked at her dumbfounded and slowly realized that she had forgotten the pots on the stove! I immediately rushed home. Sure enough, when I got there, the fire was still on and my meat on the stove. Frantic, I pulled it off the fire, popped open the lid, and tasted it. It was burned. Hundreds of people were going to be eating this, and the pressure of serving them buckled my knees. I prayed right there and asked God for a miracle. I had prepared everything perfectly. I balanced all the ingredients, all of the heat, and it all appeared to be wasted. In my prayer, the Lord came to me and told me to take it to the park and sell it anyway. I returned to the park, and got ready for my customers.

At the front of the line were two men who were stone drunk, and they asked for the chopped beef sandwich. We hesitantly obliged. We held our breath as they ate, anxiously watching to see what they would do. The first man chewed, stopped, looked a little perplexed, then excitedly announced, "There's avocado in the beef!" He went up and down telling everybody there was avocado in our beef, but of course there wasn't. It was the miracle I prayed for! We sold hundreds of sandwiches that day before our final two customers, a pair of sober

Chapter Two: It's All in the Preparation, Prayer, and the Power

ladies, took one bite and disgustedly told us it was burned. He sent me Grace in the form of fools who couldn't taste the overdone meat, I couldn't believe it. That showed me what prayer can do.

Another time in my life I was faced with some difficult days. I didn't have a job, the church I was pastoring was struggling, and my physical condition was in bad shape. My money was funny and I was very low. Then one day the phone rang. One of my long-time pastor friends was on the other end. I was railing about my situation and sounding like Job. After a couple of minutes, he broke my rant and asked me a question. He asked me if, in all of my hurt, I'd gotten on my knees and told the Lord thank you? I was baffled. I was seeking comfort, words of encouragement, a lifeline . . . something. Instead, he asked me if I thanked God for all my troubles. It's a great question. Do we ever, in the middle of our struggle, say thank you? Satchel Paige once said, "Don't pray when it rains, if you don't pray when the sun shines." We must give thanks for the rain, storms, stars, heartaches, and pains, and it is in the middle of prayer that we must practice that praise regardless of how things are going. Praise that God is good, and He will work the purpose.

I Kings 13 shows us God was working His purpose in the prophet. By being in Bethel the prophet must have accepted the challenge and conferenced with God, which were sound examples of living out his mission. His path to that point had given him full confidence that God was with him. Oh, how sweet it is to feel the power from God! It doesn't just give the feeling of power. It gives the resolve and budding confidence. It is with the Word that the power grows. As our confidence begins to bloom and flourish, so does our power. Letdowns and setbacks are inevitable, and they may shake our confidence. However, they will not stop us because His power is infinite and it keeps going.

I Must receive power.

Just as Jesus told his disciples to wait for the power when they were praying in the upper room, and it arrived; Jesus tells us to go in power through our development in *I Must*. At Bethel, the prophet had a purpose and God had a plan. The prophet had to communicate with God to receive the purpose, to embrace the purpose, and praise the purpose. He did. Once one has prayed, the *I Must* says to go with power.

I Must Pray, I Must be Prepared, and I Must go in Power.

God keeps his promises in that when we take one step, he takes

I Must

two. We are led by faith in the direction He wants us to go. Thanks be to God, I celebrate Him in prayer and praise. His glory prepares me, and His ***I Must*** power propels me each and every day.

Chapter Three

The Challenge

Luke 22:39-42

> **39** *And he came out, and went, as he was wont, to the mount of Olives; and his disciples also followed him.*
> **40** *And when he was at the place, he said unto them, Pray that ye enter not into temptation.*
> **41** *And he was withdrawn from them about a stone's cast, and kneeled down, and prayed,*
> **42** *Saying, Father, if thou be willing, remove this cup from me: nevertheless not my will, but thine, be done.*

In growing in *I Must*, there will be challenges. We will be looking at how we are to go about meeting, exceeding, and defeating them in *I Must*.

I Must accept the challenges and work through them. In **Matthew 26:36-46**, **Luke 22:39-46**, and **Mark 14:32-42**, we see Jesus meet one of His greatest challenges in the Garden of Gethsemane. He was praying to the Father for guidance in enduring the challenges of His impending torture. He knew the end was near and that all the events in His life would pale in comparison to what was coming. Jesus looked to His disciples to pray with him, but their flesh had given way to sleep. It was there, in stillness of His isolation, that Satan's attacks were aimed at crushing Jesus's spirit as if it were a spiritual olive press. The fear Satan injected was designed to keep Him from His duty. He wished for another way to carry out His mission without having to endure the agony of crucifixion. The failure of His disciples and the extraordinary temptation were terrible challenges, but He knew they were a steppingstone to His Kingship. Thank God He succeeded. This is our example. Just as Jesus knew that He must accept His challenges and be about His Father's business, so must we.

All challenges are bumps in the road. Some are light while others are far more serious. They can be life-changers that stem from circumstances that can be either controllable or uncontrollable. Some we make out of poor choices while others are forced upon us. These severe, life-changing circumstances can enable negative events to work against us. As a child of God, it often seems that challenges always work against us, but they are actually for us. We have to trust our faith and personify *I Must* by listening to the voice in our hearts that whispers, "I can and I will overcome by Christ who strengthens me." So, in **I Kings 13**, what was the challenge? There were two: One seen and one unseen. It was evident from the outset that he was to confront Jeroboam and the city of Bethel. It was not clear that he would have to deal with a flawed prophet. I'm pretty sure the prophet could easily visualize himself standing before a king and telling him, "Thus saith the Lord," but he was less able to see the other challenges that he would have to face later on.

Similarly, we face these same kinds of challenges in our lives. In **I Corinthians 13:12**, Paul says we look through a glass darkly. In that murk, we don't know what is around the corner. However, with the spirit of *I Must* and the memory of all that Christ has done for us, we must conduct ourselves as He did in **Luke 2:49** by being about our Father's business. We must carry it in fixed, pure hearts. Living and walking with *I Must* empowers those two words to energize us physically and catalyze us emotionally to drive our mission perpetually. Thinking of driving through challenges makes me wonder how soon Moses would have quit if not for the *I Must* within. As we mentioned earlier, God used the fiery bush to speak to him in **Exodus 3:10**, telling him he must go. He had to go and tell the Pharaoh, "Let my people go." Every challenge he faced after that would spark the vision of the burning bush to ignite in his heart. He and all of the prophets had an *I Must* with the Father. So, I know without a shadow of a doubt that *I Must* is alive in us, and with it we will surmount all challenges that lie ahead.

I Kings 13:2-8

> **2** *And he cried against the altar in the word of the Lord, and said, O altar, altar, thus saith the Lord; Behold, a child shall be born unto the house of David, Josiah by name; and upon thee shall he offer the priests of the high places that burn incense upon thee, and men's bones shall be burnt upon thee.* **3** *And he gave a*

CHAPTER THREE: The Challenge

*sign the same day, saying, This is the sign which the Lord hath spoken; Behold, the altar shall be rent, and the ashes that are upon it shall be poured out. **4** And it came to pass, when king Jeroboam heard the saying of the man of God, which had cried against the altar in Bethel, that he put forth his hand from the altar, saying, Lay hold on him. And his hand, which he put forth against him, dried up, so that he could not pull it in again to him. **5** The altar also was rent, and the ashes poured out from the altar, according to the sign which the man of God had given by the word of the Lord. **6** And the king answered and said unto the man of God, Intreat now the face of the Lord thy God, and pray for me, that my hand may be restored me again. And the man of God besought the Lord, and the king's hand was restored him again, and became as it was before. **7** And the king said unto the man of God, Come home with me, and refresh thyself, and I will give thee a reward. **8** And the man of God said unto the king, If thou wilt give me half thine house, I will not go in with thee, neither will I eat bread nor drink water in this place:*

The preceding passage outlines the prophet's challenge, which was to confront a great and powerful man about God's displeasure with him. The prophet had to put down his fear and stand. The Scriptures tell us that our sound mind, not our fear, is what comes to our aid in times of challenge. We have to see what's in us, or how we measure up. Locked within our innermost selves is the power to be able to accomplish any task ahead.

Challenges are forever with us, but how we deal with them starts with our inner self. It could be losing weight, ending bad habits, or even pole-vaulting over a new bar. Whatever it is, when we have accepted the challenge, we must first check within ourselves before going forward. As we confront the hidden nuances of our beings in the midst of challenge, we unpack our truths and we begin to learn. In those places, we are provided the opportunity to visit our background and lessons learned, but it is imperative to be in a forward motion. We use our respective histories to help us deal with our futures, which is as much to say that our futures are governed by our past. If we never learn from them, we are doomed to repeat them. It keeps us ever failing to move forward. However, there is hope. Our past can help us handle our challenges. We must go forward. We must keep going no matter how hard it may be.

I learned a hard lesson in calling on **I Must** when I used to landscape yards for extra money. One day a man asked me to cut his front yard. He told me I didn't have to bring any equipment and to come early because it gets really hot when the sun rises. He asked me how much I would charge him. I told him $30. Without looking at the yard or house, I told him $30. I arrived at the residence, and the front yard alone was half an acre. When I met him at the garage, he had a push mower for me. He graciously offered me water and informed me that he would be leaving for some of the day. He knew I was a deacon and a person of integrity, but he didn't seem to care. He took advantage of me and my situation. I bowed my head and said a prayer.

By the grace of God, I cut that half-acre. It took me six hours with that push mower. Now, I had some equipment at my house that would have worked much faster, but I was stuck at the man's house with his lowly old push mower. Boy, it was a long day. At the end of it, he gave me the $30 with a $5 tip. I tell you, I went home tired! I had accomplished the clear challenge in front of me, but by the time I walked in the front door, the unseen challenge hit me. My wife was waiting patiently with a request that hit me like a silver bullet. Our newborn needed some diapers and milk and all I had was the $35. It turned out that I worked all day for some diapers and milk. I thanked God for that $35 right then and there. I could have gotten it a lot easier, but I thanked God for His provisions for my child. I made it, but how? I kept thinking **I Must**. My pant legs were torn, my hands were tired, the mower was strained, but I summoned the Lord's gift of **I Must** within and finished the job.

In looking at the challenges and subsequent victories of Jesus's temptation, the prophet's victory against Jeroboam, and the victory for my family, we see expressions of the impetus behind **I Must**. **I Must** do what the Lord tells me to do. **I Must** deny myself. **I Must** tell the devil he's a liar. **I Must** ignore the naysayers who will keep me from going where I am supposed to go. In all these, **I Must** wins the challenge.

Chapter Four

Seems Like Confidence

I Kings 13:6

> **6** *And the king answered and said unto the man of God, Intreat now the face of the Lord thy God, and pray for me, that my hand may be restored me again. And the man of God besought the Lord, and the king's hand was restored him again, and became as it was before.*

When we surmount our challenges and grow from the prayerful power sent by the Word, every step forward feels like a dynamite explosion within the heart of the believer and matures into confidence. In *I Must* there will be true confidence.

Diving back into **I Kings 13**, we see where the prophet followed his orders and stood before Jeroboam with ferocity and courage like a lion straight out of Judah. He delivered the Word, which convicted the king of his wrongs. The king was infuriated and did not hesitate to raise his hand to seize the prophet. It would have been business as usual, but this time his hand was severely afflicted. When the prophet healed the king's hand, he channeled the healing power of God, and, by doing so, received confidence in his faith.

Think about that for a minute. Think about channeling the power of God through your body with the intent of healing a corrupted regent, and then facing his constituency who is trying to persecute you. I can't help but think about all the emotions that must have come rushing to the surface: the surprise, the feelings of triumph, the ability to rebuke a king, the avoidance of both prison and death, and then to deflect a king's invitation for a feast in his honor . . . all of that combined had to have been incredible! However, the prophet did not give in to the intoxication of victory. He rather proclaimed the Word of the Lord, as confidence is nothing without the protection and power of the Word. We could write libraries on how God protects His own, and as such, a man of God must not be

I Must

in fear but of a sound mind who sees every circumstance as an opportunity. Where a commoner might see a thinly-cracked window of opportunity as a limited chance, a man of God sees a wide-open shot at destiny. When a strong norther comes bellowing in and stays for days, that chilling wind will find every crack in your house. If there is even the slightest hint of a fracture in your home, a strong wind will find it with exposing gusts. As such, a man of God must always view any crack or narrow way as an opening.

When we look at **I Kings 13:4**, we see where God issued suffering to fall on the king in the form of a withering appendage. In that moment, the king's vulnerability as a man was exposed, and he pleaded to the prophet for God's mercy. His foundation was cracked. Then, simple as that, the prophet took advantage of the opportunity to proclaim the Word, thus restoring the king's hand.

Every spiritual act, every heart-moving act builds upon a spiritual cornerstone that serves as the guide for our continued growth. We are to revere it as a miracle that drives our perseverance. This steadfast development will enliven the spiritual man with confidence. When that confidence is built, it is for greater things that lie ahead. Now, it is important to view the imminent challenges as a whetting stone. I have found that the stronger the confidence, the bigger the whetting stone, and that means the sharper the spirit. That's where **I Must** triggers the power of God, the places where it would be an easy choice to quit and wilt under the lie of impossibility. It is absolutely imperative to remember there is nothing too hard for God and He will always make a way—but we have to have confidence.

Confidence is rooted in following **I Must** by standing for what we are called to do, taking the first step towards finishing it, and allowing the developing boldness and assurance to drive us to and through the finish line—all of which is the direct result of faith that has been acted upon. It is an illuminated feeling—a radiant, blind, and doubtless level of awareness that generates full and faultless execution. That, friends, is confidence. Look at David: he knew he could take down Goliath. He had already developed a fierce level of confidence from taking down a bear and a lion as a boy—Goliath was just another drop in the bucket. Just as it did for David, confidence breeds victory in our lives.

When I played college football, we had a drill where every lineman or linebacker had to go through something called "Mean Machine." It turned timid boys into fearless men. While watching

Chapter Four: Seems Like Confidence

the "Machine" at work from the sidelines, fear would snatch the air out of our lungs and freeze our hearts. Once our name was called, we swelled what courage we had and burned through the Machine. After a few rounds, our confidence would build up, and we would be razor sharp. Our coaches' goal was to make that raging confidence soar to the point that when a running back burst through the line, we would fearlessly take the ball carrier out. Everything about that drill builds a fierce level of confidence. It details what it means to have confidence by pushing through the fear of taking that first step and working from there. As we succeed in putting one foot in front of the other, every step must be directed towards finishing. In other words, when you stand up to go, you stand up to finish. *I Must* finish.

After seasons of tested determination to finish, the refined spirit within drives us through the finish line, where there is a sense of triumph that screams, "I made it!" If we remain as obedient as the prophet in his trial with Jeroboam, our victory will sizzle. As it cools, it will add another layer of the faith and power that holds up our self-efficacy. That is the thrust that sets everything in motion. God works in strange ways. They are even stranger when He builds His people's confidence. He is always ready and willing to deliver. All we have to do is shed our weakness and ask.

I Must have confidence because people don't trust weakness—they need to not just see strength and confidence but to feel it emanating from us. If there is a hint of doubt, the broken will drain every last reserve of strength right out of our flesh. It is only the Lord's compounding love in us that grows our confidence to seize the smallest of opportunities when He moves. That is the true confidence in *I Must*.

Chapter Five

Decisions, Decisions, Decisions...

I Kings 13:7

> **7** *And the king said unto the man of God, Come home with me, and refresh thyself, and I will give thee a reward.*

Luke 7:11-14

> **7** *And he from within shall answer and say, Trouble me not: the door is now shut, and my children are with me in bed; I cannot rise and give thee.*
> **8** *I say unto you, Though he will not rise and give him, because he is his friend, yet because of his importunity he will rise and give him as many as he needeth.*
> **9** *And I say unto you, Ask, and it shall be given you; seek, and ye shall find; knock, and it shall be opened unto you.*
> **10** *For every one that asketh receiveth; and he that seeketh findeth; and to him that knocketh it shall be opened.*
> **11** *If a son shall ask bread of any of you that is a father, will he give him a stone? Or if he ask a fish, will he for a fish give him a serpent?*
> **12** *Or if he shall ask an egg, will he offer him a scorpion?*
> **13** *If ye then, being evil, know how to give good gifts unto your children: how much more shall your heavenly Father give the Holy Spirit to them that ask him?*
> **14** *And he was casting out a devil, and it was dumb. And it came to pass, when the devil was gone out, the dumb spake; and the people wondered.*

Jeroboam said to the man of God, "Come home with me and refresh yourself, and I will give a reward." Oh what a decision the man of God had to make: eating bread from his bag or the king's table? From an idealist perspective, it would be a no-brainer to suggest that the man ought to eat from the sustenance of God's provision, but the truth is we all have a raging compulsion for the finest things in life. Any one of us would jump at the opportunity to eat from the king's table, the president's, the governor's, the rich man's, the whoever's we think is greater than us. Why? Because of our blindness and the feeble nature of our human-built notions of status, we think they have the best. In our minds, it's easy to be deceived by the glimmering cutlery, exotic foods, and an ambience that we probably have never seen. The best wine, the most premium of cordials, and a feeling of unrivaled pomp: all of it sounds wonderful and insatiable, but, oh, what a temptation. As we refocus on the man of God, it's very clear he had a very difficult decision to make when it came down to receiving a secular reward for performing the non-secular healing of Jeroboam's hand.

All of us have decisions to make in our lives. It's strange how the smallest decision today becomes the biggest issue in life tomorrow. For example, we can eat high-fat food today while we're young, assuming we don't have to pay for it down the road, but, inevitably, we will. Decisions, decisions, decisions . . . **I Must** make the right decision.

When our confidence is running high and we feel God in our veins; when the blood of the Lamb is blessing our lives and the Holy Spirit is igniting our souls, everything feels alive. One of the dangers of that rhythm is that it leaves us susceptible to celebrating ourselves over He who sent to us. That overflow of confidence makes it easy to ignore the Spirit and fall when making a tough decision. When we choose to eat at the king's table, there are some who are there with us but haven't touched a crumb of their dinner. It brings to mind the book of Daniel. You see, Daniel as a little boy had a similar decision to make. He had to choose whether to eat at Nebuchadnezzar's table with the others his age or just eat beans and drink water. He didn't want to eat from the king's table because it was unclean (**Daniel 1:8-16**). He and his three friends decided to remain obedient by eating beans and drinking water. That decision proved to be the greatest decision in his life. He made the decision to sacrifice and suffer a little so that he may be blessed later. If you make a sacrifice now, you don't have to pay later. But if you take short cuts and don't work hard, rest assured, you'll pay for it later. I understand that now.

Matthew 13:18-23

> **18** *Hear ye therefore the parable of the sower.* **19** *When any one heareth the word of the kingdom, and understandeth it not, then*

CHAPTER FIVE: **Decisions, Decisions, Decisions...**

cometh the wicked one, and catcheth away that which was sown in his heart. This is he which received seed by the way side. **20** *But he that received the seed into stony places, the same is he that heareth the word, and anon with joy receiveth it;* **21** *Yet hath he not root in himself, but dureth for a while: for when tribulation or persecution ariseth because of the word, by and by he is offended.* **22** *He also that received seed among the thorns is he that heareth the word; and the care of this world, and the deceitfulness of riches, choke the word, and he becometh unfruitful.* **23** *But he that received seed into the good ground is he that heareth the word, and understandeth it; which also beareth fruit, and bringeth forth, some an hundredfold, some sixty, some thirty.*

The prophet stood before King Jeroboam and had to make the right decision. In the throes of a heated moment, how do we do that? It's found in the Word. More specifically, it's found in the parable above. We see how the seed found good soil, rocky soil, shallow soil, and the soil that nurtured it grow into a thicket of thorns. Keeping healthy soil, or a healthy walk with Jesus, produces strong faith and advances our growth to make the right decisions. Furthermore, the Bible says that He will give us wisdom freely, and the decision to listen to His consultation will help us make the decisions that are the best for our lives. Instead of leaning on our own sense of wisdom, we ought to fall upon God's wisdom from the Holy Spirit, which always prevails.

When we look at decisions, we are also looking at doors of opportunity that come in many forms. Let's say a person is faced with two closed doors and one decision to make. Usually, we are going to pick the door that is going to give us the biggest gain. A lot of times the doors look the same. The difference is one will strengthen while the other will destroy. So, what will help you make the right decision? Since both doors are closed, let us first ask who closed them? Then we must ask ourselves how we got to the place of making the choice? "Did I want to, or did life make me want to?" When we live in reaction to the world, we are not able to respond with the Word. If we trusted the Word and God got us there, then His Word says that He will make a way and direct our decision. It is submission to the Lord and the faith He gives that will open the right door, and it must be blind-love faith. If we are truly in Jesus, there is no fear because He we will never lead us to choose the wrong door. If we choose the wrong door without Jesus by our side, we will suffer through it for as long as God wills—and He has no timetable. Our faith in His love will determine how long we suffer. Praise be to God for His gift in Jesus Christ, and that we can do all things in Him.

Let's look at the man of God's decisions. He was placed before Jeroboam and told to declare, "Thus sayeth the Lord." As we mentioned, for him to even be there, he had to make the correct choices, which prove that it was a God-driven affair. All he had to do was choose to follow through with his instructions. He kept choosing correctly one door after another. Each decision was building to the moment when he denied the king's rewards. He was on fire, but even though he made the right choices in obedience, his flesh would tug at his heart, making him feel that the king's reward was better than the Father's. **I Must** obey and make the right decision.

The Bible tells us to pray on all things, and that includes even the smallest of decisions. That tells me that every single one should be taken very seriously. Some can be very difficult, but every believer should know that they are to be handled with utmost care. God had to exercise the same kind of decision-making on us. For example, because He chose to save me, it touches the life of every fellow man, woman, and child I meet. Decisions, decisions, decisions . . . **I Must** make the right decision.

Chapter Six

Listen and Obey

Once we have made the right decision, we must listen and obey. We will now further examine the actions of the man of God, a prophet who was called by God to preach a message to Jeroboam. After the prophet had made his proclamation and thus convicted Jeroboam, we see that the king had been reasoned with by the hand of God. How that happened is rooted in how we are to use the *I Must* to remember, listen, and obey.

I Must teaches us to revere our God-given ability and remember our lessons. Our brains are made of a collection of billions of cells that serve as miniature hard drives for all of our five senses. When we experience a reoccurrence of anything, we effortlessly remember how to do simple things like opening a can, or we remember what soda tastes like, or we remember the wafts of delightful aromas coming out of the kitchen. When it comes to God's Word, however, we seem to forget what's good for us. In response to that, I have learned that if I remember a scripture of the Lord, it comes to me and encourages me when I need it. If we remember the savor of God's uncompromising Word, the recollection will become abundantly clear. We can reaffirm the strength from **Philippians 4:13**. In that place, *I Must* spurs us to remember that God tells us to just live by faith, and also to remember the Lord is our Shepherd and we shall not want. When I'm in need, I remember that scripture. It all works to fix my walk right up. When we remember this, it builds us, and it motivates us, and it gives us strength.

Once we have remembered His faithfulness, we must work towards listening. It is an area that invites much turmoil in our lives in that we often fail to do it. For example, the incessant fighting in the Middle East all stems from both historical bloodlines and historical miscommunication. In the art of communication, anyone can share stories of supposed importance with one another, but it's often flat and self-serving. However, when God communicates with us, He catches our attention in such a way that our hearts suddenly soften and begin to open. As our hearts open, we begin to feel His love, and it opens our ears to hear. For some reason or another, there is always an obstacle keeping us from hearing His voice. When we are primed with our hearts wide open, our ears hear clearer. When we press through the outside noise, we enter into a communion where there is a pitch-perfect clarity. It is in that place that we can feel, hear, and cling to the message He is sending. Believe me, God has many methods of getting our attention. Once we receive the blessing of His voice, He wants us to keep listening. There are an infinite number of remedies to our lives' problems that could work if we just sober up and act on what we hear. We must follow facts, truths, right directions, and proper instructions with absolutely no room for stumbling blocks like gossip or rumors. It all boils down to faith and trust. These are the guiding lights in our lives that keep us from stepping on unseen land mines.

I Must listen.

In **I Kings 13**, the man of God was entreated by Jeroboam, who wanted to reward him for restoring his hand. The king literally experienced the amazing power of God through this nameless man. He wanted to reward the man at his table, or maybe give him something great to express his gratitude. Contrary to the king's expectation, the prophet refused and recited his instructions that he could not accept the faintest hint of hospitality while in Bethel. In affirming his duty, he had taken to the plow, and there was no backing up. Here we see where God informed His servant that the man was to accomplish specific objectives, and the servant obeyed. He was instructed to abstain from any kind of reward from anyone, including Jeroboam. He worked to follow his orders by refusing bread and water. Following his path would not just lead him to Bethel, it would lead him through it so as continue the trajectory of his *I Must*.

I Must listen.

Despite the fact that Jeroboam wanted to give, the prophet was not told to receive. All of us are taught to share our gifts as we go and to continue our journey through the checkpoints of our lives. There will be times where we will reach our breaking point, where the only way to heal is by another's helping hand. In those times, we are free to be loved, warmed, and embraced with loving care. In this case, God did not permit it.

God is particularly protective of His children. In that protection,

Chapter Six: Listen and Obey

He has taught me that it is not good to eat from everybody's table. It's difficult to discern when it is and is not appropriate to dine because there is so much deception in this world. However, the key is that God will always provide an escape. You see, He is that escape. In the case of our prophet, his key was God's voice. Most importantly, he had to listen and uphold what God was telling him. As mentioned, God told the prophet not to eat or drink in that place and not to come that way again. So after convicting Jeroboam, the prophet's mission was to move on.

To us, listening can come in the form of rejecting worldly temptation and affirming Jesus as our true treasure. When we listen to the Word, we claim Jesus. We buck the system. We look at the world and outrightly say, "I don't need a 'Benz to feel whole, I don't want a huge house, and I don't want a credit card—because He is enough, and I will follow Him." For us to be successful, we must be able to ignore the material distractions of this world to attain the ends that have been prepared for us.

Are you willing to make that sacrifice? Again, I hear the voice of Jesus in **Luke 2:49** saying, "*I Must* be about my Father's business." He is very clear when He also says in **Luke 9:23**, "You must deny yourself, and you must pick up your cross and follow Me." If we can allow our hearts to be tuned to hear those words of faith, our spiritual triumph is imminent.

Look at Bruce Wayne and Batman. When Bruce Wayne fell in the well as a child, he disrupted a mass of bats. It put him in an incredibly vulnerable place and created a debilitating phobia of bats. He had to fight his way out of the pit both mentally and physically. Before he could attack the mental obstacles, his father went down to him and pulled him from the bottom of the pit where he said, "We fall down so that we can get back up." Had he solely used mental methods to get out without asking for help, he would have been stuck there a lot longer. The lesson his father taught him would be his war cry when faced with the heroic thresholds he had to cross in order to proclaim victory. He listened, he remembered, and he obeyed. We can listen all day, but if we don't obey, it's worthless. The key to walking with God is obedience. *I Must* obey to please Him who blesses me. Obedience is the key to everything in dealing with God. We are in trouble today because of Adam and his disobedience, which means all of us have sinned and fallen short, and we must accept the fact that not one of us is righteous.

I Must

What would happen if we obeyed just for a week? What would happen if we would just stick to His plan? What would we see?

The key to **I Kings'** nameless prophet's success is not only to listen or remember, but also to obey. *I Must* obey at all costs—and not just some costs—at all costs. *I Must* obey if I'm going to be successful, no matter whose feelings I hurt or who may be let down. In order to accomplish our designed purpose, we must obey what we see and hear from the Lord in His word. Now, something to keep in mind—some say they heard from the Lord, but the devil talks, too.

For example, when God commanded Saul to destroy the Amorites, God wanted everything in the city gone—all of the cattle, all of the people, everything. Saul accepted some of his directions and performed some of what he was supposed to, but not all of what he was told. He destroyed the people but came back with livestock (**I Samuel 15:22**). Samuel told Saul that it is better to obey than to sacrifice because obedience is the ultimate sacrifice of the self. God said destroy everything. Instead Saul only destroyed some things and completely disobeyed. Syncing up our memory and ability to listen comes down to one word: Obedience. Again, God said it is better to obey than sacrifice. What's the point of listening if you're not going to obey?

As messengers of God, all of us have been given specific instructions. We are to listen to them and live them out. If there is ever any chance of revisiting our accomplished territory, we must tell ourselves, "*I Must* remember what God said to me." That's the key to achieving all our goals in life and the way to unlocking what we are designed to accomplish. Now, many of us will do our best to listen and remember, but we will still disobey and ignore what we know is right for us. So in our walk, and with the goals of our lives, we must condition ourselves to live out the invocation and proclaim to ourselves, "*I Must* listen for my instructions, and learn how to use my spiritual tools to execute His plan." And when we listen, it pays off. Listening to the right source and the right people will always pay off. One of the crimes of society is our infected ego that often comes in the form of hard-headedness. The Bible calls it being stiff-necked, and because of that, many of us have to go through experiences so that we can be broken down in order to be rebuilt and start listening. The man of God listened. He heard. He remembered. Most of all, he did it with immense strength, faith and obedience.

Chapter Seven

Trick or Truth

I Kings 13:8-9

> **8** *And the man of God said unto the king, If thou wilt give me half thine house, I will not go in with thee, neither will I eat bread nor drink water in this place:*
> **9** *For so was it charged me by the word of the Lord, saying, Eat no bread, nor drink water, nor turn again by the same way that thou camest.*

The nameless man of God is a brilliant testament to how God records his inspired Word. As I mentioned earlier, He didn't leave a name for this servant because the man represents all of us. He is nameless and mighty. He is equipped with the full power of the Word. In walking with the Word's *I Must* power we are to remain obedient and ignore our enemy. Our enemy will use every opportunity to narrow our vision in order to "trick" us by creating a web of lies. The deception will cause us to miss the full portion of our instructions and subsequent blessings.

One of God's ways of communicating with us is to leave a long trail of tiny crumbs that creates a path of simple things. You see, His Word is simplistic not only in His way of addressing us, but also the literal scope of what He means when He addresses us. Within that message is the full effect of the knowledge He intends for us to glean.

In **I Kings 13**, we see where God told the prophet not to eat, drink, or even stay, but to move along through Bethel—all excellent modes of carrying out his instructions. Now, let's explore a little further my meaning when I say "trick." Satan's job is to trick us, pure and simple, and when it comes to the Word, his job is to try and fool us by attempting to stump us with it. If we fall for the lie, our vision will then become narrowed to seek instant gratification. There we will miss God's purpose because His purposes are infinitely broad and His true gratification is best when delayed. However, we can always rest in knowing His help is always for us. Most importantly, resting in His strength equips us to be purveyors of His Word in order to serve others. God's help spreads. His works hit in a myriad of ways, and I am so glad we serve Him in an open vision—an infinitely vast vision—for He is a vast and omnipresent God. That openness will invite both His instructions and seasons of waiting and refinement. When we remain obedient through the silence, we are fed and fully developed to proclaim victory as the nameless prophet did when he confronted Jeroboam with, "Thus sayeth the Lord." Satan does not like it when we execute the will of the Father. If we successfully proclaim the Word, the enemy will do anything to disrupt our victory. It is safe to assume a monkey wrench will be thrown into the mix with the firm intent of making us doubt our God. We will be brought to our knees, but we must look up without ever giving in to the fear. It's a trick the devil will use to prevent us from reaching God's ends. We can see an example of this play out in **Numbers 20:2-13**:

> **2** *And there was no water for the congregation: and they gathered themselves together against Moses and against Aaron.* **3** *And the people chode with Moses, and spake, saying, Would God that we had died when our brethren died before the Lord!* **4** *And why have ye brought up the congregation of the Lord into this wilderness, that we and our cattle should die there?* **5** *And wherefore have ye made us to come up out of Egypt, to bring us in unto this evil place? It is no place of seed, or of figs, or of vines, or of pomegranates; neither is there any water to drink.* **6** *And Moses and Aaron went from the presence of the assembly unto the door of the tabernacle of the congregation, and they fell upon their faces: and the glory of the Lord appeared unto them.* **7** *And the Lord spake unto Moses, saying,* **8** *Take the rod, and gather thou the assembly together, thou, and Aaron thy brotheer, and speak ye unto the rock before their eyes; and it shall give forth his water, and thou shalt bring forth to them water out of the rock: so thou shalt give the congregation and their beasts drink.* **9** *And Moses took the rod from before the Lord, as he commanded him.* **10** *And Moses and Aaron gathered the congregation together before the rock, and he said unto them, Hear now, ye rebels; must we fetch you water out of this rock?* **11** *And Moses lifted up his hand,*

Chapter Seven: Trick or Truth

and with his rod he smote the rock twice: and the water came out abundantly, and the congregation drank, and their beasts also **12** *And the Lord spake unto Moses and Aaron, Because ye believed me not, to sanctify me in the eyes of the children of Israel, therefore ye shall not bring this congregation into the land which I have given them.* **13** *This is the water of Meribah; because the children of Israel strove with the Lord, and he was sanctified in them.*

Moses and Aaron's fierce argument with the Israelites is one of the greatest examples of the enemy's snares. To that point, all of their provisions had been delivered to them in ways that could have only been from the hand of God. Bread had fallen from the sky, and quail had been sent flying in from nowhere, and, all the while, Moses was a dutiful servant. He was solid in his faith and had been validated in every step. All was very well until he was faced with the devastation of his sister's death. He owed her his life for having followed him down the Nile's bank. The young lady braved the dangers of swift currents, deadly snakes, and hungry crocodiles for her brother. Her absence left Moses in excruciating grief. When we lose someone that close, someone we love that hard, it feels like we will never get over it. And Moses was forced to confront both his terrible loss and the task of meeting his people's desperate needs simultaneously. The challenge was unbearable.

Then Moses, as an obedient servant should, went straight to the Lord. When God heard Moses's prayer, He commanded Moses to speak to the people. Under duress, Moses obeyed. Once the message was delivered that water would be drawn out of a rock, the starved masses began to swell with rage at the absurdity that a rock would quench their thirst. Moses was stuck. He was being challenged physically, mentally, emotionally, and spiritually. So, instead of speaking to the rock as he was told, he smote it.

Between the first strike and the second, there was a trial in Heaven. Moses was an obedient man of the Lord that the devil tricked into ignoring orders from on High. Simply put, the trickster played a trick, and a man of God got put on trial. By grace, God sent His Spirit to move Moses to hit the rock again. In that moment, Moses was found innocent in the Spirit and the rock poured out its miraculous water flow. Moses ultimately succeeded, but he missed the greatest blessing that could have been his the first time.

He allowed the trickster to seize his blessing by using words last and violence first.

Similarly, the prophet stood before Jeroboam after having passed the first test, thinking he was all done, but the real test was ahead of him. He had something far more important than facing Jeroboam. He had to face himself. Jeroboam's offers of hospitality are the exact same deceptions that reveal our selves as our true worst enemy because we will be tricked when we ignore our God. If we can get past ourselves, we have 90 percent of the battle won.

This applies to every instant where we are vulnerable. Tricks are always a threat. Because of this it is absolutely vital that we recall **I Must**. **I Must** doesn't just get called upon for some things, it's called for everything. Again, we look to **Luke 2:49** when Jesus said, "**I Must** be about my Father's business." And in **John 4**, when Jesus also said that He must go through to Samaria where he would meet with the woman at the well. He didn't care what anyone said—not the Jews, not the Greeks, not anyone. He was on a mission about His Father's business. **I Must** is the principal thrust behind what's in front of us, and we must be 100 percent about it. Don't rest, don't drink, and don't dwell in the place that is designed to be overcome. If we get caught walking back to the place we are supposed to be leaving, we must turn heel and go the other way. That's it, and that's all. Now, when we look at this, God tells us to not only ignore Jeroboam, but anyone and everyone who may be leading us to fall into our own weakness. That's the truth, and that's where the truth resides. Is it the tricks or the truth? **I Must** follow the truth, and watch out for the tricks.

Chapter Eight

The Way It's Played

I Kings 13:11-18

> *11 Now there dwelt an old prophet in Bethel; and his sons came and told him all the works that the man of God had done that day in Bethel: the words which he had spoken unto the king, them they told also to their father.*
> *12 And their father said unto them, What way went he? For his sons had seen what way the man of God went, which came from Judah.*
> *13 And he said unto his sons, Saddle me the ass. So they saddled him the ass: and he rode thereon,*
> *14 And went after the man of God, and found him sitting under an oak: and he said unto him, Art thou the man of God that camest from Judah? And he said, I am.*
> *15 Then he said unto him, Come home with me, and eat bread.*
> *16 And he said, I may not return with thee, nor go in with thee: neither will I eat bread nor drink water with thee in this place:*
> *17 For it was said to me by the word of the Lord, Thou shalt eat no bread nor drink water there, nor turn again to go by the way that thou camest.*
> *18 He said unto him, I am a prophet also as thou art; and an angel spake unto me by the word of the Lord, saying, Bring him back with thee into thine house, that he may eat bread and drink water. But he lied unto him.*

We're now going to focus on the game of life, and how it is played in **I Must**. Life is a challenge, and every day is a new day in everyone's lives. Even while laying up in hospitals, wheeling through nursing homes, drudging through mundane jobs, or being stuck in any kind of monotonous cycle, there's always something different each day—it may be in the morning, afternoon, or night, but there is always something different about that day. When we get up every morning, we are blessed with the day, and there are many games to be played. The difference is in how we play them—how we act out and work out our routines. In Christ, it's really going to be about how the day plays spiritually. I believe the hand of God moves according to His will for the lives of His people. The spiritual game is played in the unseen spiritual battles warring behind the scenes. When we process reality with our senses, we can judge our surroundings with an empirical eye, but the Spirit of God sees through the physical appearance and into the spiritual domain much in the same the way Jesus looked through Peter when He told Satan to get behind Him in the Garden of Gethsemane.

In **I Kings 13:11**, the sons of an old prophet residing in Bethel heard of Jeroboam's confrontation with the nameless prophet who proclaimed the Word of the Lord and left the king with a publicly withered hand. There had to have been an extraordinary amount of excitement to see the man of God at work! Thunderous and fearless, he had a plan, a purpose, and a praise on his lips. There was no question he was sent by God.

After the dust had settled, the prophet's sons raced home to share what they had experienced. Their father, a self-proclaimed prophet, was supposed to be a preacher, a pastor, and an evangelist for the community. When he heard the story from his sons, he heard tell of both an expression of the power of God and the presence of a brother in prophecy. He was supposed to be a prophet that had been called and knew the ways of the Lord, but he was corrupted along the way.

I really believe in my heart that is what happens to the majority of the Kingdom's distracted workers. Strange things happen along the way, and we see it when looking again to the Sower Parable: Some seeds were devoured, some hit shallow ground and blew away, some landed among healthy soil, but were choked up, and some came up in good soil and yielded perpetually. The cost of distraction is devastating and unsustainable.

God told the nameless prophet not to eat, drink, stay, or anything because the previous man He called, the old prophet of Bethel, had failed. The old man was unable to endure the temptations of such a sin-infested environment, and his spiritual growth was choked off by the world, killing his relationship with ***I Must***. The old prophet had simply lost his way and forgotten his mission. Today, this is what it looks like when we give in to the feeble needs of our flesh and fall

CHAPTER EIGHT: The Way It's Played

victim to the desires of the world instead of looking to Christ.

After hearing of all the excitement, the old prophet wanted to pounce on the success of the new prophet and the opportunity to connect with a beloved brother. He flooded his sons with questions, trying to extract every possible detail from his excited news reporters. In *I Must*, we will meet many mouthpieces along the way, but we need to discern what we're hearing. Some of it is good news while other times it is toxic because not everyone wants to see us with *I Must*. Why? Because our presence will make them realize they got played! What a playground for Satan as he sits and watches for people along the way! The Bible says many are called, but few are chosen. *I Must* is for the chosen. It is not about swiftness, but rather endurance. Even when Christ walked from Pilot to Cavalry, He had to endure along the way. Apostle Paul was called while walking from Jerusalem to Damascus. You see, *I Must* has dangers, mountains, pitfalls, tricks, but eventually, unending joy.

Once he secured the details from his sons, the old prophet saddled an ass to go after the man of God. Why? Because he wanted to offer a reward. Here was the second round of challenges to the instructions God gave the nameless prophet. He survived the first round when he ever so dutifully rejected the king's offer. From the greatest of us to the least of us, we have the same opportunity to obey or disobey. Along the way, we much watch for the play. Players will come in different shapes, colors, and sizes.

When we look at the text, we see that the old prophet recognized the *I Must* in this new man of God. For a detached man of God to go from complacent to saddling his beast and riding it, that tells me he was charged by a false *I Must* experience. In an attempt to play the new prophet, we find the old man presenting good intentions to reward his fellow brother, but sometimes that seemingly good intent can be an unintended trap. What is good for them is not always good for us. Why? Because we are about God's business, and He has a particular job that is just for us. The Body consists of a symphony of members that excel in uniquely carved-out ways that others do not. For that reason, they excel greatly in those skills when in direct relationship with the Father.

The story suggests that this old prophet wanted to share in the new prophet's ministry, but really, Satan was playing. If the elder was the true prophet of the land, Jeroboam would have already known the will of the Lord. Instead, another came along and delivered

God's will. The old man wanted to be a part of another's work, but Satan was using that desire to play the old man.

I Must keep the game, but watch for the player along the way. ***I Must*** fight a good fight because the enemy is going to cheat along the way.

After the man of God displayed his spiritual campaign against Jeroboam in front of a field of witnesses and preached the Word to the people, we find him leaving Bethel to carry on his way. The Scriptures do not tell us where God was directing him, but he was not to return. So he hit the dusty trail just as all of us do when we must hit the road. The road, as the Apostle Paul called it, is like looking through a glass darkly. We don't know what lies ahead of us, but we still must brave the elements, for when the ***I Must*** strategically presses on our hearts and calls us into action, victory is imminent if the course is stayed.

Now the man of God walked the ***I Must*** trail, but ***I Must*** wasn't finished. He still had to completely exit Bethel. God was not clear at first about where, but the exit was commanded. We all must walk by faith and not by sight. It is a characteristic He looks for in His children. He is very pleased when His righteous follow Him. However, in our walks we sometimes encounter surface distractions that are really outrageous injustices that must be confronted.

It takes me back to Rodney King's beating at the hands of the Los Angeles Police Department. The vicious act was caught on camera, but there seemed to be a discrepancy between the simple truth of the video and how the story was spun. As life portrays itself, we see, but we don't see. We hear, but we don't hear. We feel, but we don't really feel.

The man of God walked along the dusty road and decided to rest under an oak tree. There he reminisced and thought with tired feet and a wearied soul. In his resting, he was yet unaware of someone who desired to derail him from his God-directed focus. Under that tree, a man approached him who identified as a "friend." To me, friendship is a powerful thing, as it has knitted our souls to one another since the beginning. God created man. He gave him breath and declared him a living soul. Not only is God the creator, He is the Father. He is also the best friend one could ask for. A real friend sticks closer than a brother. Real friends are there even when a brother, sister, mother, and father can't be—in some ways they are closer than blood. They have an agape love toward one another—an

CHAPTER EIGHT: **The Way It's Played**

all-encompassing love, a sacrificial love that endures perpetually. Many have grown to love their friends, but then there are those who only pretend.

The contrast between true friends and those who pretend to be brings to mind the image of twins. It's always fascinated me. There have been many whom I have met that dress alike, sound alike, and look alike. In reality, they are two very different souls. Here we see the new prophet resting, and the old prophet coming to offer him the equivalent of what would be, today, a brand new 'Benz with no cost or obligations with just the keys and a full tank. Inside, that vehicle would smell of that sweet, alluring new-car aroma. To the foolish eye, it looks perfect, but is it really? In the passage, the old man sought out the new prophet to dine with him. This reflects an intention to distract the true prophet from his job. The image of twins in the form of two prophets: one right and one wrong. We have to know what's true and what's a lie.

When we look at **I Kings 13-18**, we see the elements of deception that show what hurts us on the *I Must* trail. We must know that people pay attention. As we work our respective missions from the Lord, know that people are always paying attention. It will be clear when we are about God's business, and we might think we are in a vacuum on our own, but there is always an audience watching. This ought to give us pause to be careful while walking in *I Must*. It might only be one or two, but there are always eyes, and they have mouths, too. So you know people are also going to be talking. It might be small conversation, but someone is always going to be talking. That's why it always pays to be right—to truly walk in faith and love.

As Paul says, our conversations are to be peppered with truth. Not lies. We see where the old prophet's sons were excitedly sharing all that they had seen the prophet do for Jeroboam in **I Kings 13:11-12**. One has to imagine how that made the elder feel. So, not only will they watch and talk, some will grow envious. The Bible tells us Satan is the author of all lies. He could wear a pair of pants today and a dress tomorrow. He walks in many shapes and sizes, and his approach will always appear friendly. As such, while the prophet was under the oak tree, along came a man with a friendly demeanor. It seemed a friend was coming to bring him back into Bethel. It was actually a detour away from his mission. When we walk with friends, God will reveal to us who our real friends are. The only way to walk with God and be His friend is to conform to His ways and His mindset. Any healthy relationship we carry with a fellow human being will result in us conforming to one another's ways on some level as we learn one another's tendencies and vulnerabilities. When friendship is in a healthy place, disagreement is often brief. It is in the vulnerability that the devil will twist the most beautiful aspects of a healthy friendship to derail us from our calling. The devil will always exploit relationships to play his game.

I had a professor who once threw me off my game when I tried witnessing to him. He was not having it. He shut me down, looked at me, and laughed. Despite all of that, I seriously wanted him to know Jesus. One day, I ran into him in the mall. We sat on a bench and talked for a while. Then he hit me with something that never left me. He said that I always tried to witness to him about Christ, but my approach was wrong. He reminded me that he was the professor and I was the student, and I was approaching him too directly. He asked if we could please sit down and talk about something we both agreed on. He wanted to talk about integers, and how they purposed for a solution. More specifically, he wanted me to carve a path to Jesus by showing the connection between the spiritual parables that I knew and the mathematical parables he knew.

In the same way my professor wanted me to alter my approach, which would take me off my path, the old prophet went to his younger counterpart with a friendly invitation. He offered for the young man to come eat, drink, and stay with him, and to hedge his bets, the old man spoke in such a way the younger would understand. He claimed that the Lord had also called him to be a prophet and an angel stopped him to deliver that very message (**I Kings 13:18**). These were relating forces that engaged the spiritual sense of the younger prophet, but they were tricks of the trade.

A real friend won't stop us from carrying out our Call, but rather encourage us and tell us to get up from under our oak tree and press on out of Bethel and never return. In order to fully experience the *I Must*, we must pick friends—real friends—who can relate, enhance, and nurture our skills in a like-minded trajectory to carry out the Lord's will. Don't walk with those who want to turn us away from our mission.

For the nameless prophet, the road to Bethel was open and God was silent. He gave the prophet the freedom to choose. Sometimes we'll have to trust His sovereignty even when it feels like He isn't

CHAPTER EIGHT: **The Way It's Played**

there. So, as the man was under the tree, God was silent. The road was left open, and the devil was busy. If ***I Must*** is calling us to lose weight, keep going. If there are troubles in our families, neighborhoods, or schools, we must walk with those who will encourage us to keep going. Looking back is not for the Kingdom of God. We must play the game with integrity and in community because ***I Must*** emboldens our relationship with Jesus.

Chapter Nine

Lies, Lies, Lies

I Kings 13:14-18

> **14** *And went after the man of God, and found him sitting under an oak: and he said unto him, Art thou the man of God that camest from Judah? And he said, I am.*
> **15** *Then he said unto him, Come home with me, and eat bread.*
> **16** *And he said, I may not return with thee, nor go in with thee: neither will I eat bread nor drink water with thee in this place:*
> **17** *For it was said to me by the word of the Lord, Thou shalt eat no bread nor drink water there, nor turn again to go by the way that thou camest.*
> **18** *He said unto him, I am a prophet also as thou art; and an angel spake unto me by the word of the Lord, saying, Bring him back with thee into thine house, that he may eat bread and drink water. But he lied unto him.*

Scripture says the man of God was found sitting under an oak, where he was resting, contemplating a triumphant victory in the great spirit of the Lord. He had executed exactly what had been ordered by God. He came, he visualized, he spoke, he healed, and he conquered. He left Bethel maybe thirsty, maybe hungry, but he persevered and neither ate from the king's table nor from anyone else's. Famished after leaving Bethel, he was captured by the inviting shade of an old oak. After taking some time to rest his bones, one has to think that hunger was beginning to attack his mind with sharp pangs and doubt as to where his next meal was going to come from.

He did not realize that by faith, God fed Elijah from a brook and a flock of ravens carrying food. If only he had the patience of Job when resting under that God-given tree. Scripture says it was oak. Oak is strong tree, a tree that stands through harsh weather, no matter whether it's a flood or drought, cold or hot. Its leaves are more than capable of shielding its trunk all year round. I don't know what kind of oak, but it was God's oak. In that moment, our prophet was living in the truth. What a rest! What a time to model God's command in Joshua to meditate! However, it was also a time to dig into the Spirit because the closer we are to the will of God, the harder the road, and the easier it is to fall victim to a lie. With everything that was happening, one has to wonder which way the wind was blowing. There had to be a shift in something to coincide with such an important event. All of a sudden, the story turns from the prophet called by God to an old prophet who claimed to know God. The old man asked his sons, "Where did he go? Saddle me an ass that I may find him." His pursuit led him to the young prophet under that oak tree (**I Kings 13:13-14**). He sought to persuade the man on mission to ignore his orders and turn around. There is the lie.

The elder is persuading the younger away from a divinely inspired direction—a key part in God's story, as all of us are when following our Call—which is a very serious matter. The elder was arrogantly convinced that he could curb a true prophet from his Godly path into disobedience by inviting him to enjoy some ill-begotten hospitality. For him to make this happen, he had to lie. As individuals, Christian believers, and even believers of all faiths, we have to realize there is a truth and there is a lie. There is no in-between. People who practice lying are living a lie. Every word is a lie. A mistruth, a misspoken whatever—it's still a lie.

So this old prophet, what did he use to knock this man off course? Simple. He used Spiritual Warfare. He twisted the truth under the veil of relationship. In regards to this walk that we travel on, Paul said it best in **Ephesians 6:10-12**: "**10** Finally, my brethren, be strong in the Lord, and in the power of his might. **11** Put on the whole armour of God, that ye may be able to stand against the wiles of the devil. **12** For we wrestle not against flesh and blood, but against principalities, against powers, against the rulers of the darkness of this world, against spiritual wickedness in high places." There it is: "wickedness in high places." That's our battle. It's not the worldliness but the way of the Spirit that helps us reach our high rewards. It is very important to talk with His words, especially in the middle of a spiritual war. He loves those talks. They develop a sense of clarity, and their power is drawn from the Word. Only in that Word can we contend with the enemy.

We get a clearer idea of how the trickster engaged the prophet in Spiritual Warfare, and worked him in verse 18: " I am a prophet also as thou art." In other words, "We are brothers." Those three words shook his soul and opened his eyes and mind. When one is intimately addressed as a brother, it lowers a person's shield and breastplate. It signifies that person as someone who belongs in a familial comfort zone. It's hard to decipher who is truly a brother when a perpetrator looks, walks, and feels as if they are committed to serving the Lord and humanity. One of our first questions to ask is discerning who is a brother and who is a friend? Finding those answers is important because we have to be aware that the devil comes in different forms or fashions. He is there to detour the mission, to kill the **I Must** at all costs. He knows the reward and doesn't want any of the Father's children to receive it. He is the author and prince of all lies.

As we look at this very carefully, the elder says not only am I a prophet as though art, but an angel spake with me by the Word of the Lord (**I Kings 13:18**). This is the lie, because when God gives an order, He doesn't need a messenger. We see the elder caught in his desire to rekindle a closer, more genuine relationship with God that was used to disrupt the younger's. Maybe God did call him years ago. Maybe God sent him a message through His Word to preach to the lost worlds of Judah and Israel. Maybe he got caught in the thorns of eating from the Kings' tables, taking payoffs to be quiet, and living in fear of expressing his once sound mind. Maybe those missteps landed his seed in weaker soil. Maybe it was because of the looks of things around him. Maybe things didn't work out the way he wanted. Maybe the crowds were few and the numbers were low. Maybe the offerings weren't there. Some of us won't make it through the dry periods of our ministries. We're upset there is no money, and we say we can't make it like this. Where is your faith?! Maybe this old prophet saw the twinkling of the stars and the thunderous voice of a younger voice proclaiming the Word and the joy it had brought. I think he wanted to be near someone who carried that old fire that could rekindle his. To get that feeling back he felt he had to tell a lie.

Maybe the young prophet was at a similar juncture in his life that the old prophet once was. Maybe he was hungry. Maybe he was thirsty. Maybe he just wasn't trained well enough to listen to the holes in the elder's game that could have been windows for grace. Lies and tricks cause confusion between spiritual entities.

The old prophet lied when he said, "An angel spake to me by the

I Must

Word of the Lord." I'm here to say that God does not work in lies. We must take a hard look at our friends, our brothers, our network of acquaintances while on the ***I Must*** trail. Truth is imminent, but Satan never sleeps. Know who is with us, who is not, and where the soft spots are in our relationships. It's there the Devil loves to mess things up. We must trust and walk as sparrows fly: with our eyes up, never doubting our provision, always dodging the lies.

Chapter Ten

What If?

Often after we have had time to reflect on all that God has done for us and discern the truth from the lies, we can fall into the "What If?" game. What if I could change my mistakes? What if I could revive the withered hand of regret? What if I could dig up what I buried? What if I could replace what I've broken? What if I could heal a heart seething with hatred from something I've done? What if I could have loved a little harder when I showed no love? These thoughts come to our minds each and every day.

Many of us lay our heads upon tear-stained pillows every night because of that lingering pang left by, "What if?" Our words fall out as crippled shadows of thought, yet are tied to the emptiness we can only express in desolate silence. Only God knows what we all have been through.

The younger prophet in **I Kings 13** heard words from the elder prophet inviting him to receive food and drink. The old prophet claimed the Lord had sent an angel to share this false gospel, but in truth, it was a lie. It invoked the younger prophet of God to feel the warmth of pastoral companionship. It enraged his hunger and ravaged his flesh. He was rampant with desire to taste and be satisfied by the water that filled Samson, or to be cooled by the sweet release from Judges. Maybe even longing for the bread that David ate from the temple's altar to fill his stomach in **I Samuel**. With weakened countenance, the prophet had to be spinning Scripture to feed his immediate needs. However, he was empowered by the infinite love of the Almighty with an order to fast. In the Lord there is no loss. Sadly, he broke his covenant under the guise of thinking he was with a brother, a beloved. There he was, at the table, breaking bread, maybe eating lamb, drinking milk, or eating a piece of cheese; maybe he was also drinking from Bethel's well. In one moment he felt the flash of ecstasy, but then the sobering gravity of "What if?" began to press him into the chair.

Let's talk about "What if?" What is the man of God supposed

to eat? What is he supposed to drink as he travels the *I Must* trail? Where is he supposed to be if he's not supposed to be there? Where is he to stop when he feels the hunger of his body? What is he supposed to do?

If it's from God, whatever it is, it is from the Word and there is a mandate. Whatever that mandate, we must walk by faith that it can and will be accomplished. We have to bear in mind that after receiving our mandate, there will be a stillness. It is a silence that will reign over the moment of deliverance that feels like a void. God takes a period of time where He watches and listens. He has granted all the help needed to begin the journey, and the thorn that drives our impatience is the flesh's agonizing death into obedience. That is how He sees us through.

So what is it that will help us better understand the case of the prophet's food? Believe it or not, it's as simple as discerning what kind of food is the most appropriate. God made this an issue. He said don't eat or drink in Bethel. The old prophet saddled his ass and caught up with the young prophet under the oak tree. He lied in a small effort to entice what appeared to be hospitality. The secret of what food is good comes down to the question of what kind of food we are talking about. Prime rib? Are we talking about soft-shell crabs? Grapes and bananas? Really, what kind of food are we talking about?

The food that will feed our *I Must* and help us is God's Word. I cannot stress enough the message of **Luke 2:49** in being about the Father's business. And further, how it drives His attitude about being fed in **John 4:32-34**: "**32** But he said unto them, I have meat to eat that ye know not of. **33** Therefore said the disciples one to another, Hath any man brought him ought to eat? **34** Jesus saith unto them, My meat is to do the will of him that sent me, and to finish his work." So the man of God was hungry physically, but his soul was to feast off the victory over Jeroboam and grow a little further into the *I Must*, killing any chance for the doubts of "What if?" to foster under the oak.

God would have fulfilled his hunger in time. His real hunger was satisfied from accomplishing the Father's business. According to Jesus, we must be about our Father's business. So we can see and understand how Jesus was going day and night. He was accomplishing His Father's business, and the Father always provides for His ministry. Looking to the examples of Adam, Abraham, Moses, and

Elijah, it's very clear that the Father will always feed His children. This shows us that if we fix our hearts, our minds, and our eyes directly to His business and finish it, all of our faculties will be filled. Man cannot live on bread alone, and God will fill you with all the food you need.

In **John 4:13-14**, it tells us: "**13** Jesus answered and said unto her, Whosoever drinketh of this water shall thirst again: **14** But whosoever drinketh of the water that I shall give him shall never thirst; but the water that I shall give him shall be in him a well of water springing up into everlasting life." He will not only give us food, but also everlasting water on the trail. What if the prophet had stayed a little longer under the oak tree? What if he told the old prophet, "You lie and the Truth is not in you!" What if he just held on a little longer? Never let the "What if?" drag down your life, or the regret tear your heart. Always let the ***I Must*** say, "***I Must*** be about my Father's business, and I will finish it!"

Chapter Eleven

Playing the Fool

I Kings 13:19-22

> **19** *So he went back with him, and did eat bread in his house, and drank water.*
> **20** *And it came to pass, as they sat at the table, that the word of the Lord came unto the prophet that brought him back:*
> **21** *And he cried unto the man of God that came from Judah, saying, Thus saith the Lord, Forasmuch as thou hast disobeyed the mouth of the Lord, and hast not kept the commandment which the Lord thy God commanded thee,*
> **22** *But camest back, and hast eaten bread and drunk water in the place, of the which the Lord did say to thee, Eat no bread, and drink no water; thy carcase shall not come unto the sepulchre of thy fathers.*

While the "What If?" game can replay things that should or should not have been, most of the significant changes in our lives are unforeseen. We try to walk in seas and wade in still waters, and some still waters are deep. It's funny about the oceans and seas. We can look down into them but cannot see the bottom. Even if it's two-feet deep, sometimes we cannot see. It is in those places in our lives where life-changing events lie in wait to shatter our paradigms. They change us, and sometimes we even willingly walk into horrible situations because of them.

We see this when the prophet of God willingly went back to break bread under the supposition that he would be dining with a brother. As we look into the Scriptures, we notice a collection of peculiar events in **I Kings 13** between verses 18-22. First, a lie was told. Then the prophet disobeyed God's command to abstain from any of Bethel's hospitality. As they sat at the table, the young prophet had an instantaneous revelation. After he took that first bite, the voice from on High arrested the young man and convicted him. His disobedience incurred a harsh punishment: he lost the privilege to be buried in the tombs of the fathers, and his body would be left in the street to rot. So we find this young, impatient prophet on his **I Must** trail in a catastrophic moment of weakness.

He had a choice but acted on impulse. He rushed back to Bethel for a tainted meal. If he would have just waited a little while, God would have provided, but he disobeyed. The punishment was laid upon him, but where did the idea of "playing the fool" come in? We see it in his actions. For after receiving the invitation from the old prophet, instead of getting quiet and seeking God in a lonely place by himself, or even acting like Jeroboam after being struck with a withered hand, he listened to a man, not God. So instead of praying, instead of talking to the One who hired him, he ate and drank. Simply put, he played the fool.

He had heard the voice from on High, he very nearly had executed the mission, and yet he was so quick to forget He who sent him. One of the things that we need to understand is that when we slip and make mistakes, we must go straight to the Throne that appointed us. That is what carves our path. Our God is merciful, He is full of grace, and His loving kindness knows no bounds. We may have to follow David's example in **Psalm 51**, begging for the Father to wash, clean, forgive, and help, but we can always go to the One who hired us. He loves us and will always answer if we seek Him properly. Here, God sought after him, and when God seeks us, He rescues. The prophet's job, his duty, was to fulfill the business of his Father. However, blinded by fleshly famine, he did not stop eating or drinking. At least Jeroboam had enough sense to call on the Lord through the prophet. Yet the prophet, the man with the direct connection to the Lord still refused to call on Him. Playing the fool on a dark road is a dangerous game. We can get confused, the way can get crooked, and there are many potholes and infinitely deep valleys. In the darkness is where we need His help the most, and we must clinch His hand with all our heart. But a raging hubris will drive us into ruin.

All of us play the fool when we walk in arrogance. We can't see the light because of the trees in the forest. Our heads are hanging and our eyes are on the ground instead of looking up to the sky. **Luke 12:16-20** shows us a man who had a great harvest. Instead of sharing it, he built bigger barns for himself. After that, he said he was going to eat, drink, and be merry. Then God said, "Thou fool,

CHAPTER ELEVEN: **Playing the Fool**

this night thy soul shall be required of thee." We all are subject to making a mistake that will fatally damage our lives. I truly feel that if we look very closely at the Scripture in **Luke 16:19-20**, where the rich man and Lazarus were on stage together, we can glean that a small token of generosity could have been all the difference. All the rich man had to do was throw out some crumbs to a starving man. He could have seen the bosom of Abraham, but he didn't want to do that. On the *I Must* trail, there's not room to play.

Arrogance becomes fault and disobedience keeps us from finishing what we start. As such, the prophet loaded up, and a lion was waiting crouched and ready. This lion was the judgment of God, and it knocked him off the beast he was on and slew him. But note the ass didn't run. While the lion fatally maimed the prophet, it didn't eat him. And still, the beast did not run. There was a peace in this donkey, and there was self-control in the lion. They followed orders from on High to the letter. How could an animal follow orders and finish what was started? The lion had a conviction that is synonymous with our *I Must* attitude to attack. The donkey had an *I Must* of loyalty. If the lion can live in *I Must* and if the donkey can live in *I Must*, then what about us? We can do it. Yes we can. *I Must. I Must. I Must.*

Chapter Twelve

Where is the Finish Line?

A finish line represents the end result of a job well done. We all love them. It's like the end of a workday, and we are set to head home at five. When it's close to five, we think we're almost there. Or in a race, we can see the end off in the distance. But sometimes we miss it.

Like many men, I was on a baseball team as a boy. During a game, I crushed a ball into the outfield, and made it smooth into second base for a double. While I was on second, the next batter popped a fly ball into the sweet summer sky, and as the center fielder went to catch it, he missed. I scrambled to third and was told to run home. As I was running, the catcher pulled away from home plate, and I slid. I stood up full of athletic glory and prowess, but my glass confidence shattered when the catcher caught the ball and they called me out because home plate was covered with dirt. I thought I made the finish line, but I didn't. That day taught me one of the most valuable lessons of my life: either we finish or we're out.

As our young prophet was on his trail, mounted atop his ass, he suddenly found the taste of earth and the harsh end of the Lord's justice. At God's direction, his flesh was torn, but not eaten. And there next to him was the lion at his foot, and his ass at his head. As we look at this, it's fair to ask, "Where is the finish line?" God gives us two different examples.

Those examples are dictated by our life choices. The lion represents unfinished business. If we don't finish, then it becomes hard and brutal. It becomes an agony of pain, regret, and snubbed satisfaction. And that regret slowly erodes our minds into a compost of self-loathing filled with a carousel of "I didn't finish;" "I didn't work hard enough;" "I took the short cut;" "I took the easy way;" "I forgot." And the next thing we know, "I'm dead." Many can look back on undone schoolwork. Thoughts of "I didn't make it; I didn't graduate." What about if we had the **I Must** mentality? We would have avoided the savage lions that feast on our souls, devouring our spirit and joys. Countless souls have been mangled in the grasp of a lion when caught without the *I Must* spirit.

"**4** I must work the works of him that sent me, while it is day: the night cometh, when no man can work." (**John 9:4**) *I Must* follow John's words and work the works of Him who sent me. No one can work in the dark, and if we are stuck or incapacitated, our work is undone. However, under the compulsion of *I Must*, the drive comes like the setting of the sun to remind us to get in gear to finish before nightfall.

We see this depicted at the end of **I Kings 13** in verse **28**. The donkey that carried the prophet through Bethel and stayed despite the threat of a raging beast gives us the illustration of hard work paying off. A donkey is not a carnivorous beast. A donkey is not a complainer. A donkey does not joke in serious matters. However, a donkey will laugh and call out injustice. Donkeys show patience when carrying a heavy load. They learn to finish the work they were driven to do.

The donkey represents *I Must* and instills an emboldened drive that exclaims, "I will drive through the finish line!" What a mentality that we would love to have and share. To have the patience and the courage to press on and not backtrack while carrying a heavy burden—to persevere through debilitating hunger and thirst. All one has to do is pull a little rope to move a donkey. It wants to finish and is determined to cross that finish line.

So where is that finish line? It's in making the choice to follow our God's command. If we don't finish, our regret will be compounded, and it will consume us from the inside out.

If we do finish, there is a great reward! Satisfaction guaranteed. All eyes will be on us, filled with astonishment just as they were when the ass and lion were towering over our fallen prophet. Disobedience is a choice, regardless of circumstance or weakness. There is help, however, if we just hang on and perform the task the Lord gave us.

The masses watched all of this transpire and reported back to the old prophet about what happened to the man of God. Again, the old prophet was absent during God's proclamation. Having been the vehicle for Satan's lie, the old prophet was in a decrepit state. Despite this, he went with great courage to gather the remains of his fallen comrade. God's grace was shining on him as he secured the Lord's prophesy by not burying the fallen prophet in the tomb of his

Chapter Twelve: Where is the Finish Line?

fathers but in the foreign sepulcher of the old prophet's fathers. God showed mercy. Even under disobedience and lies, He showed everlasting mercy. God allowed the ass to remain because He wanted the body of the dead prophet to be carried away. This is an expression of love, for the body could have been ravaged and eaten, but this is a testimony to God judging and correcting disobedience.

In the young prophet's death, God also saved the elder prophet. The elder saw a great sight. By picking up his friend's dead body, he both saw the power of God and felt it drive him to bless his friend in death. With blood on his hands, he used the ass to carry his former friend to his gravesite. We see here how lies and sin gave birth to death, but in using the obedient ass to carry the dead prophet to his final resting place, the elder was saved. Here, God, in His wisdom through struggle and death, took one and saved another. If one prophet was to fall, another had to step up. That is an expression of the finish line.

With this passage as our example, the finish line for us will not be found in trifled moments of weakness but in the exact time and place His will has determined it to be. We saw the old prophet racked with a heart of sorrow when he closed with, "I want to be buried with this man, whom history said stood in front of Jeroboam and commanded, "Thus sayeth the Lord." That was his punishment for lacking obedience, for not having the *I Must* attitude.

John 19:30

> **30** *When Jesus therefore had received the vinegar, he said, It is finished: and he bowed his head, and gave up the ghost.*

I Must is for whatever we are trying to do through Him. Whether it is to lose weight, build a business, form new relationships, or most importantly, if we are trying to share the Gospel, this work will equip us. If we are trying to better our homes and marriages, if we are trying reach the heights of academia, or if we're simply working to better our lives, there is always a starting point. As Jesus declared His starting point with the proclamation in Luke, "*I Must* be about my Father's business."

Jesus used the phrase, "*I Must*" to declare what He needed to do and where he needed to go all throughout the Gospel. But when He was in the garden of Gethsemane, before Pilot and Herod; when He was beaten and spit upon; when He was carrying the cross to

I Must

Cavalry's mountain, the Holy Spirit's whisper of *I Must* was driving Him. When saving a thief on a cross, forgiving others' transgressions, issuing disciples to care for his mother, enduring the agony of going to the cross, *I Must* was in Him. *I Must* thrust Him through the end as He commended His Spirit to the Father and declared, "It is finished."

I Must, I will keep working, keep striving, and keep walking. *I Must* finish and I will announce, "It is finished!" What a wonderful, wonderful word, and what a thought to proclaim, that in everything that we do, it will bring joy! And believe me, if you want joy, the words, "It is finished" will give you an unparalleled sense of joy and accomplishment. That radiant feeling pours out of graduates upon leaving seminary, and it protects us when thoughtlessly stumbling through the devil's playground, blind to his vantage point. We are wrapped in power and sprinkled with the blood from Emmanuel's veins. The enemy will disrupt our plans and cause us to lose sight of the end, but when we are broken down and seemingly crippled by the task at hand, we must submit to the same Holy Spirit that drove Jesus and declare with Him in holy symphony, "*I Must* be about my Father's business!" and "*I Must* finish!"

About the Author

Don G. Cyphers is the Pastor and Founder of Strait Gate Fellowship Baptist Church in Elgin, Texas. Pastor Cyphers was led by the Holy Spirit to begin a new work as the founder and Senior Pastor of his modern-day church that is under the direction of an unchanging God. ("For other foundation can no man lay than that is laid, which is Jesus Christ" **I Cor 3:11; I Tim 3:15**).

Pastor Cyphers holds a Bachelor of Arts in Religious Studies from Baptist Christian College in Shreveport, Louisiana; a Bachelor of Arts in Business Management with a Minor in Religious Education from St. Edwards University in Austin, Texas; and a Master of Arts from American Seminary in Oklahoma City, Oklahoma.

www.ingramcontent.com/pod-product-compliance
Lightning Source LLC
Chambersburg PA
CBHW071756080526
44588CB00013B/2258